Slice of Life

Shradha/Reynu Shintre

BookLeaf Publishing

Presentation by *BookLeaf Publishing*

Web: www.bookleafpub.com

E-mail: info@bookleafpub.com

Illustrations and book cover by Tiana Shintre

ISBN:9789358730913

First edition 2023

DEDICATION

I Dedicate this book to all my loved ones, both living and the ones who have transitioned. My Parents, Siblings, My children and above all, My Husband, who have been my pillars of support and strength always!!!

ACKNOWLEDGEMENT

I would like to thank every experience, big and small, happy and sad, that occurred in my life and prompted me to write everything that I did. All the teachers and beings that came into my life at various points and taught me a Slice of Life

PREFACE

To Discover life is a Privilege, A Privilege I would like to share with the World through - Slice of Life!

Camouflage

Now that I am older there's so much more I
realize
When I think back, it cuts me right to size

From when I was little, maybe a foot and half
Was totally dependent, as helpless as a calf

I was fed, cleaned, entertained, and Loved
I was taught right from wrong as a way to live

Right from school work, to all the classes that I
took
You were right there, I just had to turn around
and look

Through every discomfort and illness, you were
there by my side.
Suffered and made it your own, keeping vigil
and staying up all night.

Every want, every emotion, you understood
Even my silence, my wrath, and my
temperament never your love shook.

My successes, failures, and triumphs were your
very own
Tears of happiness, sorrow, and pain have your
pure love shown

Forgetting yourself, You lived your life as mine
Hiding all your troubles, you've wanted me to
shine

I feel so humbled and grateful when I see your
beautiful face
Having you in my Life is all His Grace…

I needed not to worship an alter or go any place
For I realized it was Him Camouflaged in the
form of your face!!!

Reynu!!!!

The Lease

 I started with a little toy that at that time
brought me so much joy
And then came that bicycle and to ask for more I
wasn't coy

As I grew, there was so much that I wanted to
covet
Life revolved around video games, friends and
everything seemed all set

I had to have the latest slimmest phone
The trendiest clothes and branded shoes, I was in
that zone

Got a good job and started earning well
Had a destination wedding, with a life mate who
was swell !!

A small house wouldn't do, for that
worked,burning the candle both ends
Missed out on family time, as to the best school
the kids had to send

The more I bought and the more I owned, my
ego grew
Relationships waned, and friends remained, but
a few

And when I retired and of my life, I took stock
I reflected with a bird's eye view, with what I
discovered, I was in for a shock

What I said I owned, and what I said was Mine
It was just loaned to me for a very short time

My whole life was a lease, whose expiry I didn't
know
What was really mine were my deeds for this
life and for the next that I was to sow!!!

Reynu!!!!

The Sound of Silence

In every day's humdrum and cacophony of
sounds
I feel caught and in a way bound

I look outward at the creations of the divine
I wake up to the sound of chirping birds that
make me smile inside…

The pitter patter of the raindrops on the window
have a mind of their own
In times of reflection, to me, my inner story have
shown….

I bask with the sun and wind in my face
The blowing wind whispers messages of hope
and His Grace….

The beautiful colorful flowers are abuzz with
the bees' hum
Talks to me of happy times that were and are
still to come….

I stand by the waterfall and hear its strong
gushing sound of youth

And then the tinkling stream flows with sounds
that soothe…

The waves that crash into me speak of hurdles
that are a part of life.
In the evening, that placid sea lays calm and
shows peace is in sight…..

And then I lay all by myself, spending time
within…
And I realize the best Melody is in the Sound of
Silence- that's when I am with HIM!!! That's
when I am with HIM!!!!

Reynu!!!

Little Ideas to Escape Situations...(LIES)...

When we are little, we are taught not to lie
Watching others, temptations walk in, but to
walk the straight road, we try

A child attempts to hide his mischief
If he's caught, he'll get a scold and for days
remain submissive

Among friends, it's a common sight
With someone so close, you don't want to lose
favor and face the slight

Between a couple many a time this tool is used
Sometimes to keep peace and unfairly not to be
accused

In the workplace this is commonplace
To move up the ladder and to remain in the rat
race

It's a whirlpool this game of lies
When we speak one, then in number it only
multiplies

No matter how long, it will be discovered for
sure
To have the courage to speak and the listener to
accept the truth is the only cure !!!

After all, they are just Little Ideas to Escape the
Truth

Reynu!!!!

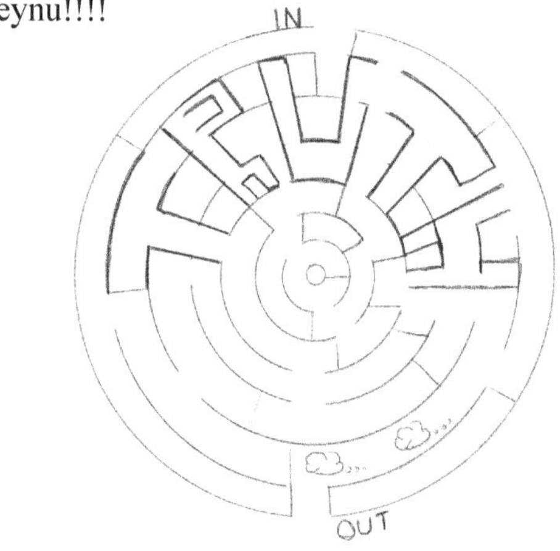

It's all Greek to Me….

When I watch a mother tirelessly look after her
little one
Go through sleepless nights and still have that
beautiful smile for her daughter or son
It's all Greek to me!!

When I see the head of the family work so hard
for everyone to provide
When it comes to his own needs, he brushes
them to the side
It's all Greek to Me….

When I see that teenager treat complete
strangers with utmost respect
But those who love him, he takes for granted so
often treats them with circumspect
It's all Greek to me….

God is not disturbed When everything in life
seems to be going well
And when times get a little tough, Him do we
blame and of every spiritual place we ring a bell
It's all Greek to me……

My waking up every morning, my heart beating
by itself
The Sun shining no matter what, His Grace
always on me is a mystery unto itself……
All in all It's all Greek to Me ….

Reynu!!!

Anger…

I gave you the earth with its pristine glory
What you did with it is another story

Gave you trees, flowers, and streams in
abundance
That gave you the air to breathe and in their
beauty to dance

Gave you fruits according to the season
That soothes you, and of discomfort there is no
reason

And what did you humans do to all my
handiwork
Amidst all your selfishness, did you once think
how hard the future generations will have to
work?

You cut down trees, ate up animals, polluted not
only air but water
Resources dried up, animals became extinct and
forests withered

I looked on in dismay, waiting for you to come
to your senses

You left me no choice except to lower my defenses

My Anger manifested in the Earthquakes,
Floods and Famines - that caused so much
sorrow
Oh Man Wake up, restore My Earth, leave
something to cherish for the children of
tomorrow !!!

Reynu !!

Memories

As I sit and reflect in solitude, in my own special
world
So many images, emotions, and experiences are
unfurled

I walk down childhood and reminisce on the
innocence
It's filled with cuddles, love, and a few scolds
needed for discipline

And what do I speak of the wonderful school
days
The beautiful teachers, the friends, the pranks - a
platform that taught values in its own special
ways

Adolescence, when I think back, sprayed a
myriad of emotions
Like a roller coaster - everything was so intense,
so important was every relation

Then I walked the bridge of adulthood that led to
the banks of maturity
Started my life with my soul mate- a meadow
with the colors of endless shades -
Responsibility and a little Serenity

In my Garden of Memories, I could weave the
most colorful tapestry
I choose to remember only the brightest and
happiest ones and ignore the ones with
Travesty!!!!

My Memories make me who I am and what I do
and where I go
So I sieve them wisely, for they map my way to
what life has still to show !!!

Reynu!!!

Music

Anything that moves me from within and keeps
me movin'
Gives me inner peace and makes me more
giving....
That's what I call Music

When I hear my little one cackle with that
innocent laugh
And when I hear the incessant chatter - it's never
enough!!!
That's what I call Music

When I get that long awaited call from my
sibling
And we exchange all the gossip and still to the
phone cling....
That's what I call Music

When with his little gestures, my beloved does
his love show
And that bantering, teasing makes the heart glow
That's what I call Music

When I spend countless hours with elders and
loving parents,

The wisdom I Glean from that sharing
That's what I call Music

And then, when I sit quietly in meditation
And hear the inner voice speak, directing me to
reflection
That's what I call Music!!!

Each one has their own Music while they're
living!
May they find the band that makes their heart
Sing
That's what I call Music !!!!

Reynu!

Ripples

The world was calm, silent, and serene.
Until I gained consciousness and everything
started seeing

The more I saw, the more I felt,
The more I experienced
Made me happy, sad, cheerful or then angr, or
incensed

On the surface, a mask I wore
Kept the storms within, not letting them come to
the fore

As time went , patience wore down and I could
take no more
A harsh word spoken, a little criticism made me
sore

Why was I becoming this person, this person I
did not like ?
An inner voice spoke : these are RIPPLES sent
to make you stronger, wiser and right..

And then I befriended these tiny ripples,
embraced them in my life

Undeterred, I plodded on, no matter what, and
smiled from within, that peace I kept in sight

Then I looked in the depths of my heart and
what did I see?
Once again, the surface was calm and clear, so
clearly my reflection I could see!!!!

And then that precious lesson I learned, life will
throw many a ripple, some big and some
small…
I have to learn to let them stay on the surface,
stay strong and never allow them to make me
Fall!!!!!

Reynu!!!

Choice

Many a time life will throw an unexpected
curveball, catching me by surprise
Forcing me to bend, fall and crumble
I know the choice is mine.... I choose to Rise.

On Many a day things can go wrong,
circumstances can try my patience, crawling
traffic can hold me back
I can curse & scream or on someone else let out
my steam
I know the choice is mine..... I choose to stay
calm , smile and take things in my stride!!

Often situations seem unfair and I feel cheated. I
worked so hard and did not get my due
I can get angry and think of ways to hurt and
take Revenge...
I know the choice is mine.. I choose to forgive,
it's not my place to God's job...
As is wont, failure and Paucity I will encounter,
Purse strings will be tight & all demands can't
be met
I can cry, I can complain and despair, I can
blame birth, time and circumstances...

I know the choice is mine.. I choose to be
grateful, bide my time, work hard knowing times
will change.....

Human nature as it is, Relationships will strain.
There will be petty fights and misunderstandings
will try to stay
I can hold back, I can be mean, I can hold
grudges & refuse to sway
I know the choice is mine... I Choose to Love, to
embrace and let bygones be bygones and save
the day...

The world can look dark, dreary and cold
The clouds can look overcast and the storm
seems endless, refusing to pass
I can get depressed and lonely and in myself
withdraw..
I know the choice is mine... I Choose to look
beyond- for the hidden Bright Rainbow , that
subdued silver lining coz when in the Almighty I
believe all the strife, problems and negativity
will have to Cease!!!!

Reynu!!

LIFE..

LIFE.....

I was walking Heaven's gates one day
You chanced upon me and swept me on the way

A little perturbed, I asked "where're you taking me?
A Map has been charted, a lot to experience and do! Soon you will see!!

With implicit trust I held your hand and with you on this journey embarked
The road seemed long, encumbered and a little dark..

Suddenly I came to bright light, cacophony of sounds & excited chatter
Where was all the silence, peace & quiet, what was the matter?

With time I was cuddled, cooed to, fed and cleaned. So often embraced- this I learned was Love

Felt so secure and soothed, like I did in Heaven
above!

As I grew in size and the mind evolved, with my
senses there was so much I explored..
With all the sights, sound & tastes I reveled,
danced & with every experience I scored!

A few years of very close bonds & then out into
the big wide world was I shown the door
Strangers became family, friends they were
called and sometimes I met dislike & this my
heart tore!

The simple world got complex, and I had to
work hard! The seed of excellence in me had to
plant
Time rushed by me, I rode the tide of grades,
successes & also of failures got a glance!

The heart was happy, had met a soulmate with
whom everything seemed right..
Felt the strength to scale mountains , hand in
hand the future looked so bright!!

The Speed of change & added responsibilities
brought on some fear mixed with ample cheer...
As age caught up I learned what's heartache as I
lost those closest & very dear!!!

As kids flew the nest & in their homes settled-
brought a state of calm
Looked inside & spent time with myself and
turned to divinity- this sure acted as a balm!!

In the slate of things, the puzzle, but for a piece
seemed complete...
What was that piece that seemed elusive, that
something that could make me replete?

Then one day, I lay as the Placid sea, you came
to see me...
"Who are you?" I asked

So many years have passed!!" Don't you
remember? I am LIFE , you see!!!"

I smiled in cognisance, The journey complete,
again we walked hand in hand - LIFE & I
He dropped me back to Heaven's gate, I thanked
him, misty eyed bid him goodbye with a
Sigh!!!!!

Reynu!!

The Mirror Me and I...

Every morning the 3 of us meet
Look into each other's eyes and each other
silently greet

The Mirror Me and I

One shows the picture as it is
The other struggles to accept what it sees
The third shows and talks to you about what's
hidden....

The Mirror Me and I

One tells of the lines, spots, and wrinkles.
The other looks in despair at what it lost through
the years.
The third reminds us of the story behind every
line and wrinkle and makes the eyes twinkle.

The Mirror Me and I

One reflects the imperfections in size and shape
The other looks with eyes downcast and sighs
over all the effort it takes
The third speaks of the beauty in the
imperfections, all that its borne and with this all
the gloom does shake

The Mirror Me and I

One shows thinned out and gray hair
The other looks away and reminisces on the
luscious curls and how good She looked in her
hay day
The third smiles and reminds her of the color
She brought to all in every way

The Mirror Me and I

One shows her how age is catching up and the
upcoming stoop
The other thinks of all the burdens and pains that
bent her so
The third boldly reminds her to stand up tall, for
all She's gained and achieved is no mean task by
far

The Mirror Me and I

And then the Three look through, and through
and together one vision see
The lines and spots, the thickened girth,the
Greys and stoops are all a sign of a life well
lived, a sign of victory
And finally the three look eye to eye and give
each other a secret smile , exchanging a message
in unison

The Mirror Me and I.

Reynu !!!

Giving

I walked down a road, and in my own world was
I
Happenstance I came across a beggar soliciting a
man with a cry.

He was shooed away and scolded for disturbing
the man
The friend of the man dips into his pocket to
give what he can

The beggar moves on to another lady of
affluence
He was greeted with a dirty look and looked on
with condescension

She haughtily reaches into her branded handbag
& gives him a note.
What prompted the charity? Pity, the need to be
left alone, or a reason to gloat?

He takes the money with his head bowed and
tears in his eyes
I know not what conflict played in his mind
under what guise

It Prompted me to think about where I stand and
what I own
Do I have a right to be in the complaint zone?

I am able bodied, have a home, food to eat,
creature comforts, and a loving family.
Filled me with Gratitude, Love for God and my
little sanctuary

I go up to the man to help him & see what more
can I do?
I realize he cannot speak and has burned soles
for the want of shoes

I look inside and feel a sense of remorse
Awakens some emotions that arise from an
internal source

I come back the next day at the very same spot
And hand him a bag of knick knacks and see the
joy this simple gift brought

I learned a very precious lesson that day
Give of what you have, give with humility,
selflessly, true joy is giving from the heart is
what I say!!!!

Reynu !!!

I am Enough..

I may not be tall and slender
I may not be a mind bender
But within me I know I am Enough !

I may not be the perfect mother
I may not know all the answers as the others
But my kids say I am Enough !

I may not keep my house spick and span
I may not be as organized, you understand
But my little space around me speaks- I am
Enough !

I may not be the best cook in the Universe
I may not spread a gourmet diverse
But the plates licked clean- tell me I am Enough
!

I may not be at the top of my career or Multi
task
I may not do things as and when I am asked
There is this little voice that says_ I am Enough
!
I may not be today's up to date socialite

I may not update statuses and tweets, every day
write
The few friends around me say- I am Enough !

I may not live in the big Bungalow my neighbor
lives in
I may not have the fanciest car that's come in
My modest four walls that keep me safe tell me I
am Enough !

When I was growing up, I am remembering the
lessons I gleaned
Do not compare, do not despair, every seed has a
time and season..
Sooner or later your time will come, remember
to tell yourself- I am Enough !

I have come in with a purpose, that with time
will be revealed
With each day I have to discover little by little
with what I have to deal
For when God sent me down- in my ears He
whispered - you are and always will be
Enough!!!!

Reynu!!!

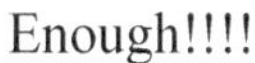

COVID

COVID came into our lives out of the blue
Agreed it's dangerous, but it taught us a thing or
two

A person of every age befriends technology &
Internet in every home zoomed
Virtual parties, video calls, and online games
mushroomed :)

Schools and Tuition classes went online
Became a tad troublesome for teachers to keep
the children in line

With all the humans locked inside
Nature was refreshed, and from traffic, there was
respite

Families bonded and connected over meals,
movies, and board games
With masks sanitizers and what have you,
nothing seemed the same

With our mouths covered, we learned to speak
with the eyes
The Namaste replaced the handshake, and with
countries strengthened ties

With Work from Home and time at hand, each
one honed and polished their skills
With gardening,cooking, baking, and the like,
life was filled

Learned to value relationships and all things
small
To respect the NOW, forget bygones, pick up the
phone, and make that call

I have Learned my lessons now, Go Corona Go
Will live with the New Normal, I have become a
better human being I Will Show!!!

Reynu!!!

The Forest

There once was a majestic forest, so green, and
so thick
"No one or nothing can do me any harm" was
it's constant think

And within that huge Grove was a small island,
as it were
Of a myriad of strong wooded trees, little shrubs
and saplings, together they had nothing to fear

Over the years,they grew in strength and in
numbers
Those were happy times, swaying and swishing
in the wind, making memories to remember

Until one Day there came a storm so strong, so
fierce - everything in its path was destroyed
Centuries of majesty brought to its knees by a
stroke of Nature, with everything it toyed

But that little island not only survived but stood
tall with pride
When asked how this came about? What was the
secret? How did they take the storm in their
stride?

Very simple, said the wise wooded trees
Our roots are bound together low down below,
where no one sees

We were protected in the shade of the older and
bigger ones said the smaller ones
We were sure we would be looked after,so we
swayed together and in unison as their sons

How did the little shrubs and saplings
survive,how did that come to pass?
Theirs, my friends, was the answer that stole my
heart.

When times are tough and there is nowhere to go
That's the time to know your true strength,to use
wisdom, to know when to surrender, the time to
leave ego behind, and to lie low.

This little island taught me about strength, unity
and fortitude

It taught me about humility and love in all its magnitude!!!

Reynu!!

The Balance...

This is a story of a mother, a son and his wife
One has looked after him, and the other has
dreamed about him all her life....

He has become who he is due to everything she
taught
Loved to the core by both, he feels blessed and
sometimes between the two caught

One has given her life, her all, forgetting her
very existence
One has left behind her world and looks to him
for sustenance

One has given him the the tastiest, yummiest
traditional treats
The way to a man's heart is through his stomach-
with a new dish every evening him does she
greet

One has set her life a certain way, at this age
difficult to expect her to change
One has come into a new world and every word
and action she tries to gauge

She knows she has handed me to another, all she
expects is a little time, thought, and care
She has to learn that she has her prince because
of her and it's only fair to share

He has to be responsible and find a delicate
balance between the two
Make a beautiful blend of old and new,
treasuring both and giving each their due!!!

Reynu!!

Who Am I ?

Who Am I ?

Am I this body that I am so attached to
Or Am I everything that I do ?

Am I - a Mother, Daughter, Sister, Friend or
Wife ?
Or Am I this Ego that causes so much Strife

Am I Defined by what is Mine and what I own
Or Am I all the successes about what I
constantly Drone ?

Am I just the reactions to all my senses ?
Or Am I a slave to all my emotions ?

After much reflection I think I am Just a spark of
God that flickers within
A spark that expands with emotions of Love,
Kindness, Generosity that to God are akin!!

I am what He sent me down to be - a reflection
of Himself
I have to dust out the conditioning, false mantles
and the like to once again find myself!!!
Reynu!!!

The Transition

I am growing at such a fast pace
As if my body parts are in a race

Oh !My favorite adidas sweatshirt and my well
worn Nike Shoes
My beautiful pink skirt in which I loved to
cruise

And what should I say about my moods and my
temper
And my tongue which is no longer in control,
many a times makes me whimper

So caught up am I in pleasing my friends and all
the peer pressure
That I don't think about the ones that have had
my back all along and who have always, me
treasured

I don't like hugs and kisses in public no more
I wish mommies would keep the love they have
for the   indoors!!

I can be real mean at times, I have realized
Sometimes I need to be put in my place and cut
to size

I am officially not an adult nor am I a child,
what can I say about my woes!!
Old enough to do house chores but can't watch
my favorite shows

My phone is like an extended body part
Instagram, snapchat and Facebook make up for a
run in the park

My tummy seems to have a mind of its own
Without a warning it starts rumbling, it's always
in the hungry zone

I am in such a rush to experiment and experience
I need speed breakers to absorb things of
relevance

I am in the phase of transition like changing
from caterpillar to butterfly you know
In a few years I will be the best version of
myself and will look back and say "Was I really
so ??!!"

This is to everyone around me, I am not totally
in control...
Bear with me, understand me and forgive me
until my raging hormones settle and on me stop
taking a toll!!!

Reynu!!

I KNOW

Life is Like the colors of the rainbow
Sometimes we are high and sometimes low
But through it all you will be there, 'I KNOW'

I may be stubborn, angry or vain
And on a bad day, I maybe a real pain
Through all my idiosyncrasies, you will keep me
sane, 'I KNOW'

When everything has been topsy turvy through
the day
With explanations none and nothing to say
In spite of your problems you will keep my
sorrow at bay, 'I KNOW'

When times have been unduly hard and tough
And the roads have been bumpy and rough
Together these roads with ease we will traverse,
'I KNOW'

In moments of happiness tears I cannot hide
Through every achievement you have been by
my side
In these special moments your eyes reflect a
silent pride,'I KNOW'

With half the journey complete and the other
half unknown
The best colors of life have yet to be shown
You will show me the colors in their best tones,
'I KNOW'

When my hair will turn gray and my gait will be
slow
But with serenity, wisdom, and love, my face
will glow
Coz with you by my side, old I will grow,'I
KNOW'

This confidence of 'I KNOW"

Is in essence True Love 'I KNOW'

Reynu!!!

I am a woman

I am a daughter,a sister,a mother, a wife
But above all, I am who I am.
I am a Woman...

I look delicate and fragile, easy to manipulate,
easy to break..
But I can withstand the pain of childbirth, and
inside I have nerves of steel...coz
I am a Woman...

I can be soft, docile and calm like a placid Sea
But if rubbed the wrong way,it won't take me
long to become the fiercest lioness you will ever
see,,..coz
I am a Woman...

I can be a cook,a teacher,a chauffeur,a friend,a
guide
But I can also be a CEO, an author,an artist,an
entrepreneur on the side coz.,,
I am a Woman,,...

I can be turned to for serious advice and can sit
up and talk all night..

But I can also be funny, naughty,crazy and full
of life coz
I am a Woman....

I was sent down with a purpose,to Love,to
nurture,a beautiful world to create.
All I need in return is Love, Respect, a little
pampering and to be valued coz
I am a Woman!!!!

Reynu!!